A Guide to
AMERICAN STATES

Puerto Rico

ISLE OF ENCHANTMENT

www.av2books.com

AV² provides enriched content that supplements and complements this book. Weigl's AV² books strive to create inspired learning and engage young minds in a total learning experience.

Your AV² Media Enhanced books come alive with...

Audio
Listen to sections of the book read aloud.

Key Words
Study vocabulary, and complete a matching word activity.

Go to **www.av2books.com**, and enter this book's unique code.

Video
Watch informative video clips.

Quizzes
Test your knowledge.

BOOK CODE

P 4 5 2 1 7

Embedded Weblinks
Gain additional information for research.

Slide Show
View images and captions, and prepare a presentation.

AV² by Weigl brings you media enhanced books that support active learning.

Try This!
Complete activities and hands-on experiments.

... and much, much more!

<hr/>

Published by AV² by Weigl
350 5th Avenue, 59th Floor
New York, NY 10118
Website: www.av2books.com   www.weigl.com

Library of Congress Cataloging-in-Publication Data

Goldsworthy, Steve.
 Puerto Rico / Steve Goldsworthy.
    p. cm. -- (A guide to American states)
 Includes index.
 ISBN 978-1-61690-811-9 (hardcover : alk. paper) -- ISBN 978-1-61690-487-6 (online)
1. Puerto Rico--Juvenile literature. I. Title.
 F1958.3.G65 2011
 972.95--dc23
                           2011019241

Printed in the United States of America in North Mankato, Minnesota

052011
WEP180511

Project Coordinator Jordan McGill
Art Director Terry Paulhus

Photo Credits
Every reasonable effort has been made to trace ownership and to obtain permission to reprint copyright material. The publishers would be pleased to have any errors or omissions brought to their attention so that they may be corrected in subsequent printings.

Weigl acknowledges Getty Images as its primary image supplier for this title.

Contents

AV² Book Code 2

Introduction 4

Where Is Puerto Rico? 6

Mapping Puerto Rico 8

The Land.......................................10

Climate...12

Natural Resources..........................14

Plants...16

Animals...18

Tourism...20

Industry 22

Goods and Services 24

Native Peoples...............................26

Explorers and Conquerors 28

Early Settlers.................................30

Notable People 32

Population 34

Politics and Government.................36

Cultural Groups 38

Arts and Entertainment..................40

Sports 42

National Averages Comparison..........44

How to Improve My Community........45

Exercise Your Mind!.......................46

Words to Know / Index....................47

Log on to www.av2books.com............48

San Juan is one of the oldest cities in the western hemisphere, but it has a modern port. The port's piers can accommodate ocean-going cruise ships and large cargo vessels.

Introduction

Puerto Rico is a unique part of the world. Situated in the Caribbean Sea, completely separate from the North American mainland, it is a tropical island paradise, featuring both bustling cities and natural beauty. As its nickname says, it is an enchanting place.

Puerto Rico is also fascinating. It has a colorful history that dates back thousands of years. It has known war and revolution. Its culture is a unique blend of the traditions of several different peoples, including its native peoples and those who came to the island from Spain, Africa, and the United States. For a long time, Puerto Rico was a colony of the Spain, and Spanish remains its main language, although English is also spoken.

The festival called carnival, just before Lent, is a time of colorful masks and costumes in the city of Ponce.

Mangrove trees line the shore at the Cabo Rojo National Wildlife Refuge on Puerto Rico's southwest coast. The protected area includes many types of tropical plants.

Puerto Rico became part of the United States in 1898, after the Spanish-American War. Although it belongs to the United States, Puerto Rico is not a state. It is called a **commonwealth**, and it has the status of what is known as an unincorporated territory. This means that although it is controlled by the United States, it is not considered a part of the United States in the same sense as a state. People in Puerto Rico, for example, do not get to vote in U.S. presidential elections. Still, Puerto Rico has many similarities to a state. For instance, it has an elected governor, and it is subject to federal laws. Its **constitution** guarantees its citizens fundamental rights, such as freedom of religion, speech, and the press, as well as the right to "life, liberty and the enjoyment of property."

Where Is Puerto Rico?

Puerto Rico is located in the northeastern corner of the Caribbean Sea among the dozens of tropical islands making up the West Indies. It lies between the Dominican Republic to the west and the U.S. Virgin Islands to the east. Puerto Rico actually is an **archipelago** of several islands. They are the main island of Puerto Rico and the islands of Vieques, Culebra, and Mona, as well as a number of smaller islands. The main island is the smallest of four large islands known as the Greater Antilles. The others in the group are Cuba, Jamaica, and Hispaniola, an island divided between the countries of Haiti and the Dominican Republic. The main island of Puerto Rico lies about 1,000 miles southeast of the coast of Florida.

Vieques is one of a number of small islands around the main island of Puerto Rico. Its eastern end is a nature preserve that includes coastal mangrove wetlands, inland forests, and coral reefs.

The Spanish saw Puerto Rico as a key location during the early years of Spain's exploration and conquest of the **New World**. Throughout the 16th, 17th, and 18th centuries, Puerto Rico was an important military post and a gateway to Cuba, Mexico, and South America.

Sailing from Spain, Columbus and his crew had been at sea for more than two months before becoming the first Europeans to come ashore in the Caribbean.

In Spanish, the name *Puerto Rico* means "Rich Port."

The first European to sail the Caribbean Sea was the Italian-born explorer Christopher Columbus. In 1492, while sailing on behalf of Spain in search of a route to Asia, Columbus discovered the islands of the Bahamas, Hispaniola, and Cuba. Spain eventually claimed most of the islands in the Caribbean Sea.

Puerto Rico is one of several U.S. unincorporated territories around the world. Others include Guam and the Northern Mariana Islands in the Pacific Ocean and the U.S. Virgin Islands in the Caribbean.

The riches obtained by the European colonizers in the New World attracted pirates, such as Captain William Kidd, to the Caribbean. The pirates attacked settlements and ships.

Mapping
Puerto Rico

The main island is shaped roughly like a rectangle. Its maximum length from east to west is 110 miles. The maximum distance north to south is 40 miles. Puerto Rico is made up of 78 municipalities, or *municipios*, including one for Vieques and one for Culebra. These municipalities are in some ways similar to counties in U.S. states. They are divided into barrios, or neighborhoods.

Mona

Sites and Symbols

SEAL
Puerto Rico

FLAG
Puerto Rico

OFFICIAL FLOWER
Puerto Rican Hibiscus

OFFICIAL BIRD
Stripe-headed Tanager

OFFICIAL TREE
Kapok

Nickname Isla del Encanto ("Isle of Enchantment")

Motto *Joannes Est Nomen Eius* ("John Is His Name")

Song "La Borinqueña," words by Manuel Fernández Juncos and music attributed to Félix Astol Artés

Acquired by United States December 10, 1898

Capital San Juan

Population (2010 Census) 3,725,789

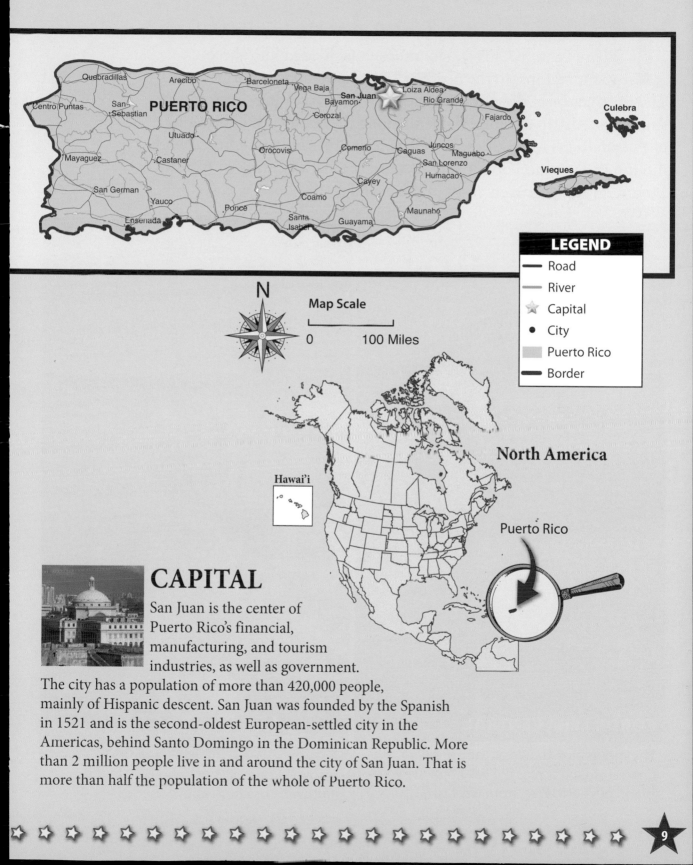

LEGEND

- —— Road
- —— River
- ☆ Capital
- ● City
- ▮ Puerto Rico
- ━━ Border

N

Map Scale

0   100 Miles

North America

Hawai'i

Puerto Rico

CAPITAL

San Juan is the center of Puerto Rico's financial, manufacturing, and tourism industries, as well as government. The city has a population of more than 420,000 people, mainly of Hispanic descent. San Juan was founded by the Spanish in 1521 and is the second-oldest European-settled city in the Americas, behind Santo Domingo in the Dominican Republic. More than 2 million people live in and around the city of San Juan. That is more than half the population of the whole of Puerto Rico.

The Land

The main island accounts for almost all of Puerto Rico's land area of about 3,425 square miles. It is divided into three main regions. In the north is a region that has soft limestone. The rock has been dissolved in places by water, creating caves and sinkholes. A strip of rather flat land along the coasts is the location of Puerto Rico's main cities, as well as beautiful sandy beaches. A wide mountainous region dominated by the Cordillera Central, or Central Mountain Range, covers most of the island.

CORDILLERA CENTRAL

The mountains known as the Cordillera Central stretch across the length of the main island of Puerto Rico, from west to east.

CABO ROJO

The limestone cliffs of Cabo Rojo in the southwest rise high above the sea.

COASTAL PLAIN

A strip of flat land rims much of the main island of Puerto Rico, where the land meets the blue waters of the Caribbean Sea.

CULEBRA

Culebra lies to the east of the main island of Puerto Rico. Punta del Soldado is at the southern tip of Culebra.

Fierce winds and high seas from Hurricane Hugo caused severe damage in Puerto Rico in 1989.

Climate

Puerto Rico lies in the tropical climate zone. Summers are hot, and even in the winter months, the weather stays warm. The average annual temperature on the main island is about 80° Fahrenheit. Temperatures up in the mountains tend to be a bit lower than on the coasts, and the northern side of the island is generally cooler than the southern side. The Cordillera Central mountain range has a great affect on the island's weather, influencing cloud coverage and rainfall across the island. The rainy season lasts from April to November. About half of the annual rainfall comes between August and November, which is the hurricane season. The southern coast tends to be slightly drier than the northern coast. Annual precipitation is much greater in some mountain regions.

Average Annual Precipitation Across Puerto Rico

The coastal cities of Mayagüez, Ponce, and San Juan typically receive between 35 and 70 inches of rainfall a year. Why does Pico del Este get so much more?

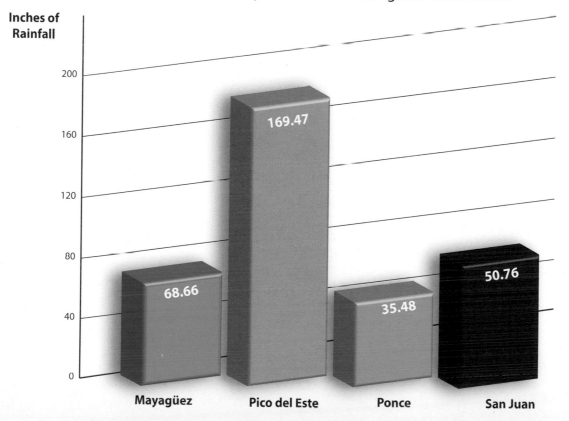

Inches of Rainfall

City	Inches
Mayagüez	68.66
Pico del Este	169.47
Ponce	35.48
San Juan	50.76

Natural Resources

As an archipelago of lush tropical islands, Puerto Rico has a number of important natural resources. It has deposits of metal ores, including copper and nickel, although they are not currently mined. There is abundant limestone, which is used to produce cement and to construct roads or buildings. Gravel makes up a major part of Puerto Rico's mineral output.

Fish farming accounts for some of Puerto Rico's fish production. Cobia fish are raised in large tanks at Culebra.

Puerto Rico still possesses lush forests, although trees cover a smaller area than before the arrival of Europeans.

One unusual natural resource on the island of Mona is seagull and bat guano, or droppings. Guano is useful as fertilizer and in making gunpowder. Mining of it began on Mona in the mid-19th century and continued until 1927.

Along the coast of the main island, salt flats have formed over the years in places where salty seawater brought by tides was trapped and evaporated. People have for centuries used these flats as a source of salt. Particularly striking salt flats are located on the southwest coast, notably in the Cabo Rojo National Wildlife Refuge.

Not all of Puerto Rico's natural wonders are found on the islands. Offshore there are huge reefs, formed by tiny organisms called coral. The reefs provide habitats for many kinds of sea life, and they are an attraction for tourists.

Many islands have vast forests of trees and underbrush. The entire island of Mona was declared an "insular forest of Puerto Rico" in 1919. It has been a protected natural area ever since. Mona is about 22 square miles in area, and it is located about 40 miles west of the main island. In 1960, park rangers were posted there to keep watch over the island's natural resources. They have conducted tours and educational camping and hunting expeditions for tourists. The island, like the rest of Puerto Rico's natural resources, is managed by the Department of Natural and Environmental Resources.

Plants

E l Yunque National Forest, located in a mountainous area 25 miles east of San Juan, constitutes the remains of a once great tropical rain forest. It has rainfall year-round, and it is the only tropical rain forest among the U.S. national forests. El Yunque is one of the oldest forest reserves in the western hemisphere. Its origins go back to the 1800s when Spain ruled Puerto Rico. The forest covers 28,000 acres.

Also noted for its diversity is Guánica State Forest, covering nearly 10,000 acres on the southwestern coast of the main island. It is one of the best examples in the Caribbean of a dry forest, which is a forest that experiences a long dry season each year. Guánica has over 700 species, or types, of plants, several of them existing nowhere else on the planet.

POINSETTIA

Puerto Rico is known as a land of colorful plants, including the poinsettia. It has clusters of bright red leaves, and small yellow flowers grow in the center of these clusters.

MANGROVE

Guánica and some other coastal areas have pockets of water-loving mangroves. These trees' dense root system and foliage protect coastal habitats from storm damage.

ORCHID

Puerto Rico is home to dozens of varieties of orchids. In El Yunque National Forest alone, more than 50 types of orchids grow wild.

FLAME TREE

Flame trees are common in Puerto Rico. Peñuelas, on the south coast not far from Ponce, has the nickname "The Valley of the Flamboyant Trees."

Puerto Rico's official tree, the kapok, was a sacred symbol for the ancient Maya of Central America. Peoples of the Amazon River region in South America used the fiber from the kapok's pods to make blowgun darts. The fiber is often used today to stuff pillows, mattresses, and even stuffed toys.

Maricao State Forest in the western part of the main island features an amazing degree of diversity. It has more than 1,100 different plant species, including more than 100 kinds of orchids and roughly 175 kinds of ferns.

Animals

The islands of Puerto Rico are home to a wide range of animals and insects. Dolphins and whales swim in offshore waters. There are about 350 species of birds and numerous species of frogs, including more than a dozen found only in Puerto Rico.

The tiny frog known as the *coquí* is Puerto Rico's unofficial state animal. It gets its name from the sound it makes, a high-pitched chirping "ko-kee." It is only about an inch in length and may be green, gray-brown, or yellowish in color.

Some animals, such as goats, sheep, and monkeys, were brought to the islands by humans, although the majority of species in Puerto Rico occur there naturally. Land animals native to Puerto Rico tend to be small in size.

BOA

Puerto Rican boas feed on bats. They hang down in front of a bat cave, often from a tree branch. When a bat flies out, the snake catches it with its jaws and then squeezes it to death.

MONKEY

The rhesus macaque and other types of monkeys were introduced to Puerto Rico by humans. Because of a lack of natural predators, their numbers increased.

MONA GROUND IQUANA

The ground iguana of Mona Island is the largest lizard native to Puerto Rico. It can grow as long as 4 feet.

COQUÍ

The little *coquí* frog is born with a tiny tail that almost immediately falls off. There are many different types of *coquí* frogs. El Yunque National Forest alone has more than a dozen species.

The pitirre, or gray kingbird, is small, but it will fight larger birds and mammals to protect its territory. It has become a symbol for Puerto Rico's independence movement.

The water in some bays has a green, blue, or pink glow at night. The colors come from tiny organisms in the water called dinoflagellates. They are too small to be regarded as animals, or as plants for that matter. They give off light through a process called bioluminescence.

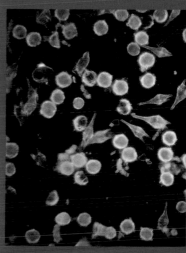

Tourism

Puerto Rico attracts tourists with its natural wonders, continually warm weather, beautiful beaches, and rich culture. The vast majority of visitors are Americans. Because Puerto Rico is part of the United States, Americans ordinarily do not need a passport to enter the islands. Many tourists come from Mexico, the Dominican Republic, and other Latin American countries, as well as from Canada. Tourists also arrive from European countries such as Spain and France and from Asian countries such as Japan. Puerto Rico has about a dozen public airports. Its ports can accommodate ships ranging from private yachts to ocean liners and cruise ships.

PUNTA HIGUERO LIGHTHOUSE

Puerto Rico has well over a dozen lighthouses. The Punta Higuero Lighthouse, at Rincón on the west coast, is now surrounded by a park and is a popular destination for visitors to the island.

EL YUNQUE NATIONAL FOREST

El Yunque National Forest is located in the Luquillo Mountains. Visitors can see more than 200 different species of trees, 150 varieties of ferns, and many hundreds of species of flowers.

OLD SAN JUAN

The Old City of San Juan, rich with history, attracts many people who visit Puerto Rico. The Spanish built forts to protect it from invaders and, in the 1700s, constructed a massive wall around Old San Juan.

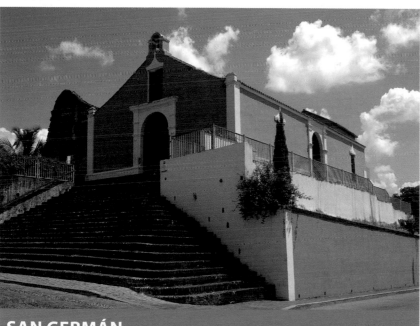

SAN GERMÁN

San Germán is an old town with many historic buildings. Its Porta Coéli Church, originally built in the early 17th century, has been restored and made into a museum of religious art.

The Teatro Tapia in San Juan is one of the oldest theaters in the Western Hemisphere. Built in the 1830s, it was named after Puerto Rican poet and playwright Alejandro Tapia y Rivera in 1937.

The Puerta de San Juan, or San Juan Gate, is one of six enormous wooden gates in the wall around the Old City of San Juan. The gates were closed and barred after sundown.

The Arecibo Observatory, near Arecibo on the main island's northern coast, is the world's biggest single-dish radio telescope. Built in a sinkhole, it measures 1,000 feet across. It has been used in the search for extraterrestrial life.

Industry

H istorically, farming was the main industry in Puerto Rico. Sugarcane was the most important crop. The growing of sugarcane gave rise to a liquor **distillation** industry that still thrives in Puerto Rico today. Puerto Rico is known around the world as a top producer of rum. Sugarcane is no longer a major crop, and Puerto Rico imports sugar to make its rum and other products.

Industries in Puerto Rico
Value of Goods and Services in Millions of Dollars

Tourism is a major factor in the Puerto Rican economy. It provides jobs for many people in various industries. Which industries is it most likely to affect?

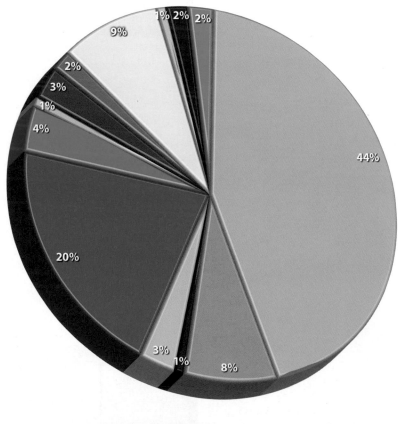

LEGEND

Agriculture, Forestry, and Fishing	$613
* Mining	$62
Utilities	$2,115
Construction	$1,929
Manufacturing	$40,548
Wholesale and Retail Trade	$7,343
Transportation	$999
Media and Entertainment	$2,618
Finance, Insurance, and Real Estate	$18,845
Professional and Technical Services	$3,224
Education	$749
Health Care	$3,183
Hotels and Restaurants	$1,778
* Other Services	$373
Government	$8,762
TOTAL	**$93,141**

*Less than 1%. Percentages may not add to 100 because of rounding.

Today, manufacturing is far more important than agriculture. In the San Juan area there are numerous factories that produce clothing, metal goods, cement, refined sugar, tobacco, and food products. Puerto Rico also makes medical drugs, chemicals, electronics, and machinery.

Thousands of Puerto Ricans work in the pharmaceutical industry.

Luis Muñoz Marín International Airport in San Juan is the busiest airport in the Caribbean. It averages about 10 million passengers a year.

Puerto Rico is about 8 hours by plane from Los Angeles. It is 3½ hours by plane from New York City.

About 5 million people visit Puerto Rico each year, coming by plane and by boat.

The Puerto Rican economy relies heavily on exports to the mainland United States and to other countries. Each year, its exports and imports combined are worth more than $100 billion.

Goods and Services

In 1947, government officials decided that the best way for Puerto Rico's economy to grow and provide jobs was **industrialization**, the creation of industries that manufacture goods. They began a massive project called "Operation Bootstrap." This involved using incentives such as tax breaks to persuade U.S. companies to build factories in Puerto Rico. Manufacturing soon began to play a more important role than agriculture in the Puerto Rican economy. Puerto Rico imported fuels and raw materials, made products in its factories, and then exported them.

Operation Bootstrap and later programs to increase manufacturing in Puerto Rico created jobs for construction workers as well as factory workers.

Bananas are one of Puerto Rico's most important crops.

Puerto Rico's main trading partner is the United States, which receives more than 70 percent of its exports. The next most important trading partners are Germany, the Netherlands, and Belgium, but they account for only a few percent each.

Major pharmaceutical companies with factories in Puerto Rico include Johnson & Johnson, Merck, Pfizer, and Smithkline Beecham.

More than 30 million gallons of distilled liquor, such as rum, are exported from Puerto Rico each year, most of it to the United States.

Puerto Rico uses oil, as well as some natural gas and coal, to make most of its electricity. These energy sources are all imported. Puerto Rico gets a small amount of electricity from water power. It also uses solar power and wind power.

Today, Puerto Rico's exports include everything from chemicals, electronics, and clothing to fruit juice concentrates, rum, and canned tuna. Medical drugs, or pharmaceuticals, and medical instruments and equipment play a leading role among the products Puerto Rico exports.

Key food crops include coffee, pineapples, plantains, and bananas. Puerto Rico also produces poultry, dairy products, and other livestock products.

Manufacturing makes a huge contribution to the economy, but most Puerto Ricans work in service industries, holding jobs in places such as banks, stores, offices, hotels, and health-care facilities. Tourism is a major source of service industry jobs in Puerto Rico.

Native Peoples

There is evidence that people may have been in the Puerto Rican archipelago as early as 6,000 years ago. Some scientists think they may have come from the region of what is now Belize in the Yucatán Peninsula. Around 4,000 years ago people from the Orinoco region of present-day Venezuela in South America began settling in the archipelago. Later peoples to arrive in Puerto Rico came from South America. These peoples spoke languages belonging to a group called Arawak. The people called the Saladoids seem to have been good farmers. Pottery and jewelry made by them have been found, along with flat plates, or griddles, that were used to make bread from the cassava plant.

The Indigenous Ceremonial Park at Caguana near Utuado on the north coast includes examples of ancient rock carvings called petroglyphs.

The Tibes Indigenous Ceremonial Center near Ponce features a burial ground, ancient ball courts, a museum, and a re-creation of an Indian village.

According to Christopher Columbus, the Taino language was "gentle, the sweetest in the world, always with a laugh."

Many English and Spanish words come from the Taino language. English examples include *barbecue, canoe, hammock, hurricane, sweet potato*, and *tobacco*. The corresponding Spanish words are *barbacoa, canoa, hamaca, huracán, batata,* and *tabaco*.

In the Taino language, the word *Taino* means "good people."

A ball game called *batos* was popular with the Tainos. Teams of 10 to 30 people used a small rubber ball and played in a rectangular court in the middle of their village. Sometimes conflicts between tribes were settled with a game of *batos*.

By around 1200 AD, an Arawak-speaking people known as the Tainos dominated Puerto Rico, which they called "Borinquen." That name came from the Taino word *Borikén*, which means "Land of the Valiant Lord." Some scientists think the Tainos developed from earlier groups living there. Other scientists suggest the Tainos came from elsewhere. Whatever the Tainos' origin, they had a well-organized society. Tainos were either *naborias* (commoners) or *nitaínos* (nobles). Their leaders, who could be male or female, were chiefs called *caciques*. Their shamans, or holy men and women, were known as *bohiques*. Shamens were thought to have healing powers and to able to talk with the gods.

The Tainos were experienced farmers and grew squash, beans, corn, peppers, and sweet potatoes. Their most important crop, however, was yucca, or cassava. The Tainos were also expert seafarers. They traveled from island to island to fish and hunt. Many Tainos lived in large villages called *yucayeques*. People lived in large round houses, or *bohios*, made from wood, straw, and palm leaves. A *bohio* might hold as many 10 to 15 families.

San Juan was a busy port in the 17th century.

Explorers and Conquerors

The first European explorer to set foot in Puerto Rico was the Italian Christopher Columbus. Sailing under the flag of Spain, he first came upon land in the New World in October 1492, in the Bahamas. He made another voyage the following year. On November 19, 1493, he landed on an island that he named San Juan Bautista, which is Spanish for "Saint John the Baptist." Several years later the island's main city received the name Puerto Rico, meaning "Rich Port." Soon after, this city and the island switched names.

Spain ruled Puerto Rico for about four centuries. Over the years, European countries such as France, England, and Holland attempted to take the Puerto Rican archipelago, but Spain retained control.

In 1898 war broke out between Spain and the United States. Fighting took place in the Western Pacific and the Caribbean, including an invasion of Puerto Rico by U.S. troops. The Spanish-American War lasted only a few months. Then came negotiations on a peace **treaty**, which was finally signed near the end of 1898. As part of the treaty, the United States gained possession of Puerto Rico.

Timeline of Settlement

Early Civilizations

Around 4000 BC Humans are present in Puerto Rico. They create rock carvings called petroglyphs.

Around 1200 AD The Tainos dominate the archipelago.

Spanish Rule

1493 Christopher Columbus lands on an island that he names San Juan Bautista but is now known as Puerto Rico.

1508 The first Spanish settlement in Puerto Rico, called Caparra, is established by Juan Ponce de León.

1509 Ponce de León becomes Puerto Rico's first governor.

1868 An unsuccessful rebellion against Spanish rule begins in the town of Lares. This uprising is now known as El Grito de Lares, or "The Shout of Lares."

1898 From April to August, fighting occurs in Puerto Rico and elsewhere during the Spanish-American War.

U.S. Possession

1898 On December 10, Spain and the United States sign the Treaty of Paris, which gives the United States possession of Puerto Rico.

1917 Puerto Ricans receive U.S. citizenship.

1947 Operation Bootstrap gets under way, bringing industrialization and economic growth.

1948 Luis Muñoz Marín wins Puerto Rico's first democratic election for governor.

Early Settlers

Spanish settlers began to arrive shortly after Christopher Columbus came to the region. In 1508, Juan Ponce de León established the first settlement, calling it Caparra. The Spanish built towns with farms, churches, and schools. They forced the native, or **indigenous**, Taino people to work in the fields, at building sites, and in gold mines. The Tainos' attempts at rebellion were put down.

Map of Settlements and Resources in Early Puerto Rico

4 *Puerto Rico's first mill for grinding sugarcane, powered by oxen, is built in 1523 at what is now Añasco. In the following years, other mills are built in many places along the south and west coasts.*

1 *Juan Ponce de León founds the first European settlement, called Caparra, in 1508, but the settlers soon move to a nearby site, today's San Juan, that is easier to defend.*

5 *In the 1500s the Spanish mine small deposits of gold at Daguao and elsewhere. Within a few decades the gold is nearly all gone.*

2 *San Juan, given the formal name of San Juan Bautista de Puerto Rico in 1521, lies on a wonderful natural harbor, enabling it to become a major military outpost and shipping center for the Spanish.*

6 *Ponce, today one of Puerto Rico's biggest cities, is founded by the Spanish in 1692, in an area that was a major ceremonial site for the indigenous people.*

3 *San Germán, Puerto Rico's second-oldest town, is founded in 1511.*

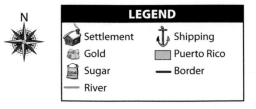

LEGEND		
Settlement	Shipping	
Gold	Puerto Rico	
Sugar	Border	
River		

The Tainos also suffered from diseases brought by the Spanish from Europe, such as smallpox. The Tainos had no natural immunity against these illnesses. Within a few decades, an estimated 90 percent of the Taino population had died as a result of violence and disease.

In 1513, Spanish settlers started bringing African slaves to Puerto Rico to replace the dwindling Taino population. Spain did not abolish, or end, slavery in Puerto Rico until 1873.

Around 1515, the Spanish also brought sugarcane. For hundreds of years afterward, growing sugarcane played an important role in Puerto Rico's economy. The first sugarcane farm was at Hato Rey.

The Roman Catholic Church was very influential in the territories held by Spain. Alonso Manso in 1511 became the first bishop appointed to Puerto Rico. His arrival there a couple of years later made him the first bishop to set foot in the New World.

Juan Ponce de León came to the New World with Christopher Columbus on Columbus's second voyage, in 1493. Before becoming governor of Puerto Rico, he served as a military commander and deputy governor in Hispaniola. He explored Florida in 1513. He is buried in San Juan Cathedral.

I DIDN'T KNOW THAT!

Time and again Puerto Rico was attacked by pirates and military forces eager to seize its wealth or to take control of its strategic position. As a result, the Spanish made San Juan one of the most heavily fortified cities in the New World. The first fort built was La Fortaleza, or "The Fortress," constructed in the 1530s. It is now the residence of Puerto Rico's governor.

In 1539 the Spanish began construction of Fort San Felipe del Morro at the entrance to San Juan Bay. Called El Morro, it has walls as thick as 25 feet.

The largest of all the Spanish forts at San Juan, and the biggest **fortification** in the entire New World, was the Castillo de San Cristóbal. Built in the 17th and 18th centuries, it has walls and lookout towers that rise more than 150 feet from the sea.

Notable People

Puerto Ricans are often referred to as *boricuas* and *borincanos*, names derived from the Taino words *Borikén* and *Borinquen*. They are a talented and proud people who have made many contributions to their home of Puerto Rico and the world at large. They have excelled in fields ranging from politics to law, entertainment, and sports.

LUIS MUÑOZ MARÍN (1898–1980)

Originally an advocate of independence, Muñoz Marín developed into a key supporter of commonweatlh status, which combines some degree of self-government and association with the United States. He ran for governor in Puerto Rico's first democratic election for the post, in 1948, and he won. He was later twice reelected. Before becoming governor, he served as president of the Puerto Rican Senate and pushed for the economic modernization program known as Operation Bootstrap. Many people consider him the father of modern Puerto Rico. In 1963 he received the U.S. Presidential Medal of Freedom.

SILA MARÍA CALDERÓN (1942–)

Calderón was the first woman to be elected governor of Puerto Rico. Before serving as governor, from 2001 to 2005, she held such public offices as the governor's chief of staff, Puerto Rico's secretary of state, and mayor of San Juan. She was a member of the Popular Democratic Party, which favors keeping Puerto Rico's commonweath status.

SONIA SOTOMAYOR
(1954–)

In 2009, Sotomayor became the first Hispanic person, and only the third woman, to serve on the U.S. Supreme Court. Born in New York City to Puerto Rican immigrant parents, she studied law at Yale University. After graduating, she worked as a New York City assistant district attorney, a lawyer, and a federal judge.

LUIS FORTUÑO
(1960–)

A native of San Juan, Fortuño was elected governor in 2008. The victory was the biggest win ever for his pro-statehood New Progressive Party. Earlier in his career, he worked as a lawyer and in public service. He then represented Puerto Rico for four years in the U.S. House of Representatives, where he was aligned with the Republican Party.

JOSEPH M. ACABA
(1967–)

The California-born Acaba was the first person of Puerto Rican descent to become an astronaut. He took a Puerto Rican flag along with him on a March 2009 space shuttle flight. During that flight, he served as a mission specialist and performed two spacewalks. He is scheduled for a tour of duty on the International Space Station in 2012.

I DIDN'T KNOW THAT!

Rita Moreno (1931–), a singer, dancer, and actress, earned the Academy Award for supporting actress for her performance in the 1961 movie *West Side Story*. She is the only Hispanic Oscar winner to also receive Emmy, Tony, and Grammy awards for her work in TV, theater, and music.

Roberto Clemente (1934–1972), a right fielder, played his entire Major League Baseball career with the Pittsburgh Pirates. He led the National League in batting four times and was the league's Most Valuable Player in 1966.

Population

The main island of Puerto Rico is the smallest of the four islands of the Greater Antilles, but it does not have the smallest population. Jamaica has fewer residents. In 2010, Puerto Rico had a population of more than 3.7 million people. In the 16th to 18th centuries, immigrants to Puerto Rico were generally Spaniards or African slaves. In the 19th century, people also came from other European countries and from other parts of Latin America. Today, African Americans make up roughly 7 percent of the Puerto Rican population. People identified as American Indians, primarily Tainos, account for only a fraction of 1 percent, but the number of people with partial Indian ancestry is much larger.

Puerto Rico Population 1950–2010

Puerto Rico had about 1.5 million more people in 2010 than in 1950. As an area's population grows over time, what actions might its government need to take to meet the needs of a greater number of residents?

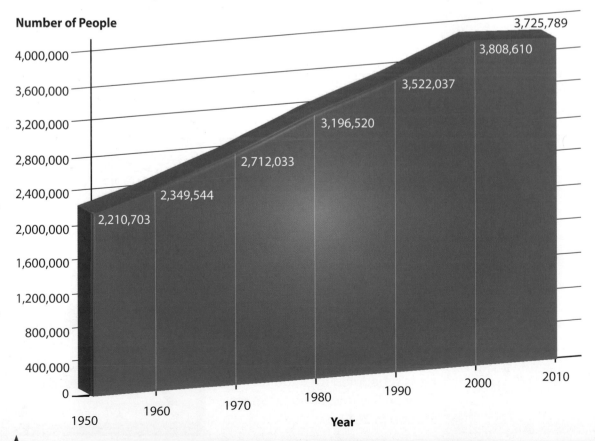

Number of People

- 2,210,703 (1950)
- 2,349,544 (1960)
- 2,712,033 (1970)
- 3,196,520 (1980)
- 3,522,037 (1990)
- 3,808,610 (2000)
- 3,725,789 (2010)

Year

More than 11 percent of Puerto Rico's population lives within the city of San Juan. The Puerto Rican capital has more people than all but about 40 cities on the U.S. mainland.

Since the 1960s, people from the Dominican Republic have accounted for the largest share of immigrants to Puerto Rico. Cubans have made up another major immigrant group, especially in the 1970s and 1980s.

Beginning in the 1940s, many Puerto Ricans have moved to the mainland United States in search of better jobs and economic opportunities. Most have settled in the New York City area or Florida. After a long history of continuous increases, the 2010 Census found that Puerto Rico's population had dropped slightly between 2000 and 2010. People moving to the mainland was one factor in the decline. Another important factor was a falling birthrate. In 2010 the annual birthrate in Puerto Rico was estimated at 11.42 births per every thousand people, down from more than 20 in the early 1980s.

Politics and Government

Puerto Rico is subject to U.S. federal laws, but its only representative in the U.S. Congress is a nonvoting delegate to the U.S. House of Representatives. This delegate is called a resident commissioner. Under its constitution, adopted in 1952, Puerto Rico is called a commonwealth. The commonwealth is self-governing, but the U.S. Congress has final authority over it.

The Puerto Rican government has three branches. They are the executive, legislative, and judicial. The executive branch is responsible for carrying out Puerto Rico's laws and for performing most administrative functions of the government. It is headed by the governor, who is elected to a four-year term.

Puerto Rico's capitol is the building where the legislature meets. It was completed in 1929, except for the dome, which was finished more than three decades later in 1961.

The current Mayagüez city hall was built after the previous building was destroyed by an earthquake in 1918.

The legislative, or law-making, branch has an elected legislature with two parts. One part, called the Senate, ordinarily has 27 members, and the other part, known as the House of Representatives, usually has 51. If a party wins more than two-thirds of the seats in the Senate or House of Representatives, the minority receives additional seats to raise its share up to one-third. Members of the Senate and House of Representatives are elected to four-year terms.

The judiciary, or court system, is headed by the Supreme Court. The Supreme Court has seven members, who are appointed by the governor, subject to approval by the Senate. They can remain in their positions until the age of 70.

Puerto Rico's official song is called "La Borinqueña."

The song is in Spanish. Here is an English translation:

The land of Borinquen where I have been born. It is a florid garden of magical brilliance.

A sky always clean serves as a canopy. And placid lullabies are given by the waves at her feet.

When at her beaches Columbus arrived, he exclaimed full of admiration: Oh! Oh! Oh! This is the beautiful land, that I seek.

It is Borinquen the daughter, the daughter of the sea and the sun. of the sea and the sun, of the sea and the sun, of the sea and the sun, of the sea and the sun!

Cultural Groups

Puerto Rico's cultural groups are a diverse and dynamic mix from around the world. Immigrants from such places in Europe as Germany, Scotland, and Ireland have brought some of their traditions and customs. Strong influences have come from neighboring Caribbean nations, such as Cuba and the Dominican Republic, as well as from the United States and South America.

The largest cultural influence in Puerto Rico is Spanish, either directly from Spain or from other Latin American countries. This influence is reflected in Puerto Rico's music, the architecture of its towns and cities, its visual arts, and its values and customs. Catholicism, brought by the Spanish, remains the chief religion in Puerto Rico, and some of the most important annual celebrations and traditions are connected with Christian religious holidays, such as Easter, Christmas, and Three Kings' Day, or Epiphany.

Dominoes, which became popular in Spain in the 1700s, is now one of the most widely played games in Puerto Rico and other places in Latin America.

Most **anthropologists** agree there are no full-blooded Taino people living anywhere today. People claiming to be of Taino descent most likely are a mixture of Taino, Spanish, and African heritages. A 2002 study suggested that more than 60 percent of Puerto Ricans may have genetic links to the Taino people. Elements of Taino culture survive in Puerto Rico. They include some traditional methods of farming, fishing, and using medicines. Groups such as the Jatibonicu Taino Tribal Nation, the Taino Nation of the Antilles, and the United Confederation of Taino People seek to preserve Taino culture.

The African slaves taken to Puerto Rico by the Spanish beginning in the 1500s brought their customs, rituals, and art. They had a rich history of oral storytelling. Puerto Rico's style of music called *bomba* evolved from the African tradition of drummers with hand drums and dancers challenging one another with their rhythms and movements. Another type of music influenced by African culture is *plena*, which includes elements from other cultures as well. In addition to a small hand drum, it often features use of an instrument called the guiro, believed to have originated with the Tainos. In its traditional form the guiro is made by hollowing a gourd and cutting notches on one side. It is played by scraping it with a stick. The *baquiné*, a traditional ceremony held after the death of a child, may have come from Africa, although some experts think it may have Spanish origins.

In some local festivals, especially at carnival time, people called vejigantes wear colorful masks and costumes.

Arts and Entertainment

Music and dance are in the hearts of the Puerto Rican people. Puerto Rico boasts a rich variety of musical styles. They feature a mix of rhythms and melodies from Africa and Spain, combined with influences from other Caribbean communities and the United States. In addition to *bomba* and *plena*, there are other types of folk music. These include *seis* and *decima*, which have roots in Spain. Influenced by jazz from the United States, Puerto Ricans developed a distinctive form of Latin jazz. Jazz is also one of the roots of salsa, which enjoys great popularity in Puerto Rico. Hip-hop and electronica beats, along with Latin sounds, can be heard in Puerto Rican reggaeton, which probably evolved, at least in part, from Jamaica's reggae.

Singer and actor Ricky Martin was born Enrique Martín Morales in San Juan. He first gained attention as a member of the Puerto Rican boy band Menudo and went on to record the extremely successful 1999 single *Livin' la Vida Loca*. His album sales as a solo artist total more than 60 million worldwide.

José Ferrer was a distinguished stage and screen actor and director. Born in the Santurce area of San Juan, he was the first Puerto Rican to receive an Academy Award for best actor, which he won for the 1950 film *Cyrano de Bergerac*. In 1985 he became the first actor to receive the National Medal of Arts. Another Santurce native who earned an Oscar is Benicio Del Toro.

Benicio Del Toro won an Academy Award for best supporting actor for his role in the 2000 film Traffic.

Several major figures in U.S. and Puerto Rican music and entertainment come from the Puerto Rican community in New York, including Tito Puente and Marc Anthony. Puente, known as "The King of Latin Music," brought the Cuban mambo and Latin jazz to the clubs of New York City in the 1950s and 1960s with his sensational drumming on the timbales. He composed more than 450 songs and recorded over 100 albums. Singer and songwriter Marc Anthony is the biggest-selling salsa artist in history.

Marc Anthony and his wife, Jennifer Lopez, are both New York–born entertainers of Puerto Rican heritage. Lopez has built a successful career as a singer, dancer, actress, and businesswoman.

Sports

Puerto Ricans enjoy many spectator sports. Boxing, volleyball, and basketball are among the more popular ones, but the dominant sport is baseball. Puerto Rico does not have any Major League Baseball teams. Its highest-level professional teams play in the Puerto Rico Baseball League, which operates during the months when it is cold in most of the United States. The Puerto Rico men's national baseball team has competed in the World Cup of Baseball many times. The team won the gold medal in 1951. As of 2010 it had earned the silver and bronze four times each. Many Puerto Rican baseball players have gone on to play in Major League Baseball in the United States. Pitcher Hiram Bithorn, from Santurce, became the first Puerto Rican to play in the major leagues when he took the mound for the Chicago Cubs in 1942.

Felix "Tito" Trinidad was one of Puerto Rico's best boxers ever. He won world titles at the welterweight and middleweight levels.

Jockey Angel Cordero's thousands of wins included three victories in the Kentucky Derby and four in the Breeders' Cup.

Standout softball pitcher Lisa Fernandez was born in New York City to a Cuban father and Puerto Rican mother. She won three gold medals with the U.S. women's softball team in Olympic competition. In the 2000 Olympics she set an Olympic record for strikeouts in a single game, with 25.

Anita Lallande is a former Olympic swimmer from San Juan. She holds the record for most medals won at the Central American and Caribbean Games. She won a total of 17, including 10 gold, between 1962 and 1966.

Puerto Rican jockey Angel Cordero, Jr., had one of the greatest horse-racing careers ever. He registered his first win in 1960 in Puerto Rico and began racing in the United States two years later. By 1992, when he retired, he had accumulated 7,057 wins. He was inducted into the Racing Hall of Fame in 1988.

International sporting events provide Puerto Rico with an opportunity to gain world recognition for its achievements. It takes part in such events, including the Olympics, separately from the United States.

Puerto Ricans began playing baseball while still under Spanish control. In 1897 there were three teams in San Juan.

In its first game at the 2004 Olympics at Athens, Greece, the Puerto Rican men's national basketball team pulled off a stunning upset. Led by Carlos Arroyo, it defeated the U.S. team, 92–73. The loss was the worst ever in Olympic play for the highly favored U.S. team, which was dominated by star National Basketball Association players.

National Averages Comparison

The United States is a federal republic, consisting of fifty states and the District of Columbia. The United States also has a number of unincorporated territories, including the commonwealth of Puerto Rico. Today, the United States of America is the third-largest country in the world in population. The U.S. Census Bureau takes a census, or count of all the people, every ten years. It also regularly collects other kinds of data about the population and the economy. How does Puerto Rico compare to the national average?

Comparison Chart

United States 2010 Census Data *	USA	Puerto Rico
Admission to Union	NA	December 10, 1898
Land Area (in square miles)	3,537,438.44	3,424.56
Population Total	308,745,538	3,725,789
Population Density (people per square mile)	87.28	1,087.96
Population Percentage Change (April 1, 2000, to April 1, 2010)	9.7%	−2.2%
White Persons (percent)	72.4%	75.8%
Black Persons (percent)	12.6%	12.4%
American Indian and Alaska Native Persons (percent)	0.9%	0.5%
Asian Persons (percent)	4.8%	0.2%
Native Hawaiian and Other Pacific Islander Persons (percent)	0.2%	—
Some Other Race (percent)	6.2%	7.8%
Persons Reporting Two or More Races (percent)	2.9%	3.3%
Persons of Hispanic or Latino Origin (percent)	16.3%	99.0%
Not of Hispanic or Latino Origin (percent)	83.7%	1.0%
Median Household Income	$52,029	$18,314
Percentage of People Age 25 or Over Who Have Graduated from High School	80.4%	25.4%

*All figures are based on the 2010 United States Census, with the exception of the last two items.

How to Improve My Community

Strong communities make strong states. Think about what features are important in your community. What do you value? Education? Health? Forests? Safety? Beautiful spaces? Government works to help citizens create ideal living conditions that are fair to all by providing services in communities. Consider what changes you could make in your community. How would they improve your state as a whole? Using this concept web as a guide, write a report that outlines the features you think are most important in your community and what improvements could be made. A strong state needs strong communities.

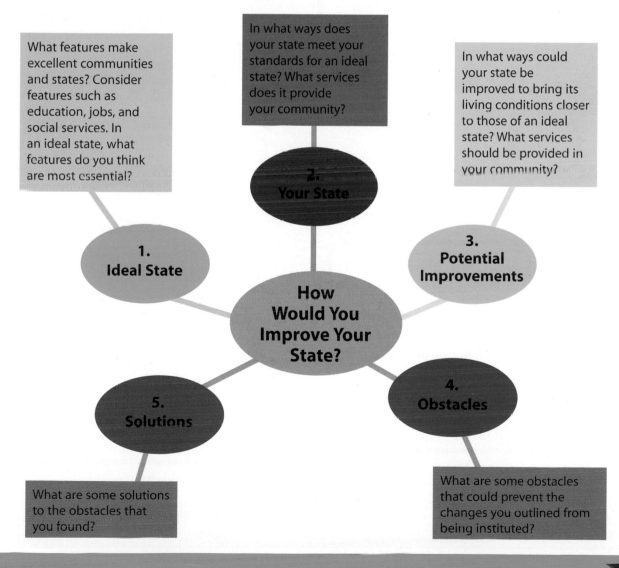

What features make excellent communities and states? Consider features such as education, jobs, and social services. In an ideal state, what features do you think are most essential?

In what ways does your state meet your standards for an ideal state? What services does it provide your community?

In what ways could your state be improved to bring its living conditions closer to those of an ideal state? What services should be provided in your community?

2. Your State

1. Ideal State

3. Potential Improvements

How Would You Improve Your State?

5. Solutions

4. Obstacles

What are some solutions to the obstacles that you found?

What are some obstacles that could prevent the changes you outlined from being instituted?

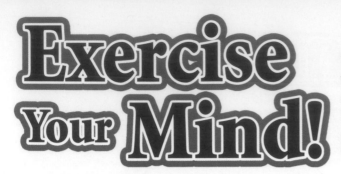

Exercise Your Mind!

Think about these questions and then use your research skills to find the answers and learn more fascinating facts about Puerto Rico. A teacher, librarian, or parent may be able to help you locate the best sources to use in your research.

1 Who was the first European to reach Puerto Rico?

2 When did the first European to reach Puerto Rico arrive there?

3 What is the name given to a group of islands, such as those that make up Puerto Rico? What group of islands in the Pacific is a U.S. state?

4 What does *Puerto Rico* mean in English?

5 What is the unofficial animal of Puerto Rico?

6 What is the capital city of Puerto Rico?

7 Who were the people living in Puerto Rico when the first Europeans arrived?

8 What future American president became a military hero for his actions during the Spanish-American War?

Words to Know

anthropologists: scientists who study the origins and cultural development of peoples

archipelago: a group of islands clustered together

commonwealth: an outlying region that has a degree of self-government but is associated with the United States, such as Puerto Rico or the Northern Mariana Islands in the Pacific

constitution: the set of basic laws that determine how a country, state, or commonwealth is governed

distillation: a process involved in making rum or other types of liquors

fortification: the act of fortifying a city, that is, building a fort to protect the area

indigenous: referring to a group of people who are natives of a particular region

industrialization: the process of creating industry in a particular region, that is, going from a farming community to a manufacturing, factory-based community

New World: the Americas, in contrast to the Old World consisting of Europe, Asia, and Africa

Nuyoricans: residents of New York City who are of Puerto Rican descent

treaty: a formal written agreement signed under international law between independent countries

Index

Acaba, Joseph M. 33

Anthony, Marc 41

Arecibo 21

Arroyo, Carlos 43

Bithorn, Hiram 42

bomba 39, 40

Calderón, Sila María 32

Caparra 29, 30

Captain Kidd 7

Casals, Pablo 41

Clemente, Roberto 33

Columbus, Christopher 7, 27, 28, 29, 30, 31

coquí frog 18, 19

Cordero, Angel, Jr. 43

Cuba 6, 7, 35, 38, 41, 43

Culebra 6, 8, 11, 14

Del Toro, Benicio 40

Dominican Republic 6, 9, 20, 35, 38

El Yunque National Forest 16, 17, 19, 20

Fernandez, Lisa 43

Ferrer, José 40

Fortuño, Luis 33

Hispaniola 6, 7, 31

kapok tree 8, 17

Lopez, Jennifer 41

Martin, Ricky 40

Mona 6, 15, 19

Moreno, Rita 33

Muñoz Marín, Luis 23, 29, 32

Operation Bootstrap 24, 29, 32

plena 39, 40

Ponce 5, 13, 17, 27, 30

Ponce de León, Juan 29, 30, 31

Puente, Tito 41

San Germán 21, 30

San Juan 4, 9, 13, 16, 21, 23, 28, 29, 30, 31, 32, 35, 40, 41, 43

Sotomayor, Sonia 33

Spanish-American War 5, 28, 29

Tainos 27, 29, 30, 31, 32, 34, 39, 41

Trinidad, Felix 42

Vieques 6, 8

Log on to www.av2books.com

AV² by Weigl brings you media enhanced books that support active learning. Go to www.av2books.com, and enter the special code found on page 2 of this book. You will gain access to enriched and enhanced content that supplements and complements this book. Content includes video, audio, web links, quizzes, a slide show, and activities.

Audio
Listen to sections of the book read aloud.

Video
Watch informative video clips.

Embedded Weblinks
Gain additional information for research.

Try This!
Complete activities and hands-on experiments.

WHAT'S ONLINE?

Try This!	Embedded Weblinks	Video	EXTRA FEATURES
Test your knowledge of the state in a mapping activity.	Discover more attractions in Puerto Rico.	Watch a video introduction to Puerto Rico.	**Audio** Listen to sections of the book read aloud.
Find out more about precipitation in your city.	Learn more about the history of Puerto Rico.	Watch a video about the features of Puerto Rico.	**Key Words** Study vocabulary, and complete a matching word activity.
Plan what attractions you would like to visit in Puerto Rico.	Learn the full lyrics of Puerto Rico's song.		
Learn more about the early natural resources of Puerto Rico.			**Slide Show** View images and captions, and prepare a presentation.
Write a biography about a notable resident of Puerto Rico.			
Complete an educational census activity.			**Quizzes** Test your knowledge.

AV² was built to bridge the gap between print and digital. We encourage you to tell us what you like and what you want to see in the future.
Sign up to be an AV² Ambassador at www.av2books.com/ambassador.